The Superbook of
FLAGS

George Beal

KINGFISHER BOOKS

Contents

This edition published in 1986 by Kingfisher Books Limited,
Elsley Court, 20–22 Great Titchfield Street, London W1P 7AD
A Grisewood & Dempsey Company
Reprinted 1987
© Grisewood & Dempsey 1986

BRITISH LIBRARY CATALOGUING IN PUBLICATION DATA
Beal, George
   The superbook of flags.
   (Kingpins)
   1. Flags—Juvenile literature
   I. Title
   929.9'2   CR101

ISBN 0-86272-193-8

Cover design by the Pinpoint Design Company
Typeset by Southern Positives and Negatives (SPAN), Lingfield, Surrey.
Printed in Hong Kong

Cover: Flags flying at the Maracana Stadium in Brazil.

Previous Page: A monument in Washington D.C. commemorates the raising of the American flag on the Pacific Island of Iwo Jima during the Second World War.

Flags

Flags are so common that we barely notice their existence. Every day we see flags flying from the roofs of important buildings and churches, and decorating all kinds of objects, from tee-shirts to tea trays. Flags appear on many special occasions. In military parades, soldiers carry them with great solemnity. On festive occasions, they are seen in strings decorating streets and buildings, and waved by enthusiastic crowds of people. Flags are essential equipment on board a ship, and are constantly flown both at sea and in port.

Clearly flags are important objects. They are used throughout the world as a means of identification and communication. Above all, they are regarded as symbols, of nationality, religion, politics and ideas. People have carried these symbols to distant and inaccessible places, from the tops of the highest mountains, to isolated islands in vast oceans. Flags have been taken into space on the bodies of spacecraft. Together with illustrations of the flags of all the countries of the world, this book describes the history of flags, the purposes they serve, and the ideas they represent.

Early Flags

Flags and banners have been part of human history from the earliest times. It is not known where, or when, the flag was invented, or for what purpose its makers intended to use it. Many of our distant ancestors, in different parts of the world, probably came up with the idea at about the same time, discovering that an animal skin, or some other object attached to a stick, could create a useful means of signalling.

Ancient civilizations possessed and used flags of various kinds. The flag as we know it today, a large piece of cloth flown from a pole, was created by the Chinese as long ago as 3000 BC. Such flags were made of colourful silks and were used by armies and during religious celebrations. But other types of flag were also developed by the ancients. Banners known as vexilloids were devised by peoples living in Asia. These were not made of cloth, but consisted of solid emblems, made of wood, metal, leather or some other material, fixed to a staff, and often represented the gods. When carried into battle, these banners were believed to offer protection and victory to the army.

Ancient European civilizations used flags for similar purposes. At the sea battle of Salamis in 480 BC, the Greek commander

Top left: A bronze and silver standard from Asia Minor, 2300 BC. Top right: An Iranian vexilloid, 5000 years old. Above left: A primitive vexilloid, and right, an Egyptian vexilloid of about 3200 BC.

Themistocles inspired his fleet to a famou victory by hoisting a red cloak on an oar an carrying it into battle. The Romans, like th ancient Asian peoples, carried standards the thought of as sacred. At first, different legion used different animals as emblems, but afte 104 BC the eagle standard, called the *aquila* wa used throughout the empire. Later, portrait of the emperor were added to the standard, t remind conquered peoples of the might of th Romans.

Early Chinese Flags

China has flown flags for thousands of years. As long ago as 1122 BC, a scribe wrote that the ruler of that time, the Emperor Chou, always carried a white flag before him when he was in a formal procession. There were many other kinds, often with a dragon emblem, a device which conveyed the idea of wisdom, not fear. Flags often bore stripes, or were shaped as shown in the pictures.

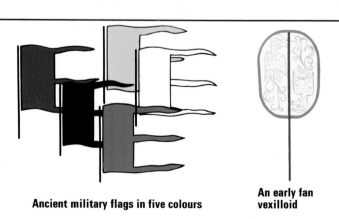

Ancient military flags in five colours

An early fan vexilloid

Some Roman Standards

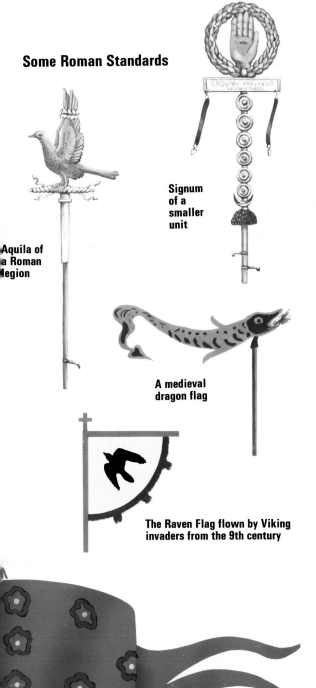

Aquila of a Roman Legion

Signum of a smaller unit

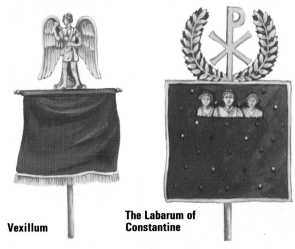

Vexillum

The Labarum of Constantine

A medieval dragon flag

The Raven Flag flown by Viking invaders from the 9th century

The Oriflamme of Charlemagne

The standard of Genghis Khan displays his personal emblem, a gyrfalcon

After the Roman emperor Constantine had been converted to Christianity in AD 312, Roman standards bore the Christian symbols *X* and *P*. Three hundred years later, the followers of a new religion, Islam, founded by Muhammad, adopted a green turban with black and white banners as their symbol, and green remains a distinctive colour in the national flags of many Islamic nations to this day.

During the Middle Ages, many famous flags appeared in Europe. One was the historic bright orange-red flag carried by King Charlemagne, called the *Oriflamme*. A second was the dragon flag, shaped like a windsock and often painted to look like a flying dragon. A device which whistled when the wind blew through it was placed inside these flags, in order to terrify armies on the battlefield. Other famous flags during this period were those carried by feared leaders, such as Genghis Khan, or feared armies, such as the Vikings, whose emblem was a raven.

▶ **Black and gold banners are shown in this illustration taken from a 13th-century Islamic manuscript.**

5

Flags of the Renaissance

Over the centuries, political events became an important source of flag design. For example, the conflicting claims of the British and French during the long series of wars between them were represented on the flags they adopted. First of all, the English king Edward III placed the French *fleur-de-lis* on his royal banner, indicating his wish to see the two countries united under the English throne. This claim to the French throne lasted for many centuries, and the *fleur-de-lis* remained part of the English Royal Standard until 1801. In the 15th century, the most famous opponent of English rule in France was Joan of Arc. The white colour of her banner came to symbolize liberty, and was preserved in the French flag. It is still there, in the modern French tricolour.

Many emblems were established as permanent features of European flag design in this period. One of the longest-lasting has been the double-headed eagle, which was first used by King Charlemagne in the 9th century. From the 13th century it appeared on the golden banner of the Holy Roman Empire.

Today it is represented on the arms and flags of West Germany and Austria.

The 16th century was an age of exploration and discovery, during which flags were used to represent the claims of European nations to rule over the lands their explorers had found. When Christopher Columbus landed in the West Indies in 1492, he carried the royal standard of his patrons, King Ferdinand and Queen Isabella of Spain, and so claimed the land for Spain.

Fifty years later, the *conquistadors* Hernando Cortes and Francisco Pizarro fought campaigns in South America under personal standards. Cortes carried a plain red banner, and Pizarro an elaborate flag composed of heraldic designs and symbols.

In Europe, meanwhile, the 16th century was a period of religious wars, between Christians and the Muslims of Turkey, and between Catholics and followers of the reformed Protestant church. Elaborate heraldic standards, such as that belonging to Charles V, developed at this time. They often illustrated the triumph of one cause over another.

The banner of King Edward III of England

The flag of the Byzantine Empire

The double-headed eagle er of the Holy Roman Empire

The standard of Joan of Arc

Religious Flags

Like the totem poles made by the North American Indians, flags have often been thought of as sacred objects. The ancient Romans attached considerable religious power to their standards, first to the *aquila*, and then later to their first Christian standard, the *Labarum* of the emperor Constantine.

The Christian cross is one of the oldest and most widely used flag symbols in the world, and images of the Virgin Mary are common in Catholic countries. During the Middle Ages, armies carried flags celebrating their patron saints, in order to protect themselves and bring good luck in battle.

The green banners of Islamic countries employ many emblems, some of them in elaborate Arabic script. The most famous Islamic emblem is the crescent moon.

▶ Religious emblems: The cross of St George (top), and the Virgin of Guadalupe, a powerful religious symbol carried on processional banners in Mexico.

The flag of the Sikhs

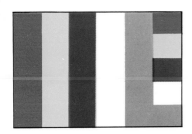

A standard flown by a grandson of Muhammad

The flag of the Buddhists

A German peasant revolt standard of the 520s (above) contrasts with the ornate lags used by King Francis I of France (above ight), and the Emperor Charles V (right) during the same years.

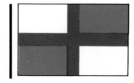

Two of the Russian flags created by Peter the Great about 1700

In medieval times, Genoa's flag showed the cross of St George

The jack of Italy

The naval ensign of Japan

The merchant flag of Israel

Flags at Sea

Flags decorate the European ships that defeated the Turks at the battle of Lepanto in 1571.

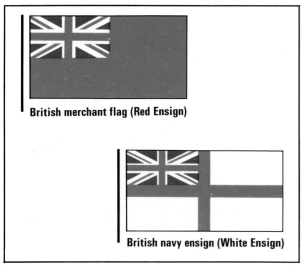

Flags have been an important method of communication and identification at sea for almost as long as there have been ships. Among the earliest were the fish emblems and tassels carried by ships in the Aegean over 4000 years ago.

In the Middle Ages, flags began to be used to distinguish between ships from different places, and between warships and merchant ships. Warships flew the banner of the king or nobleman in command of the ship, and arranged the colourful shields of the knights on board along their sides. Often, giant symbols were painted on ships' sails. Trading ships came to fly a cross at the top of their masts together with the flag of their home port, and sometimes the pennant of their owners. The flags of some of these ports became famous. Ships sailing out of ports belonging to the Baltic trading association known as the Hanseatic League flew red heraldic flags. In the Mediterranean, the emblems of Genoa and of Venice were well known.

During the 16th century, the decoration of ships became more and more elaborate. The king's ships, for example, might display enormous royal banners bearing the king's coat-of-arms from the masthead. There might also have been long streamers in the king's

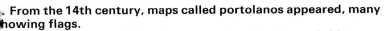

From the 14th century, maps called portolanos appeared, many showing flags.
The white crosses of Danzig appeared on the flags of ships operating from that city during the Middle Ages.

fficial colours, and, on ceremonial occasions, *avisades*, lines of official shields, were placed long the ships' sides. Ships that sailed in the Spanish Armada in 1588 would have been decorated in this manner, as would those ighting at the battle of Lepanto between the Venetians and the Turks in 1571.

As the sea-routes became busier, these omplicated decorations had to be substituted or simpler designs which made ships easier to dentify. From the 16th century, English ships adopted the red St George's cross on a white background as standard. French ships could be recognized by a number of designs, ncluding the white cross or the three gold *eur-de-lis* on a blue background. Dutch ships displayed flags composed of orange, white and blue.

At the end of the 17th century, Peter the Great, tsar of Russia, began a policy of ship-building and naval improvement intended to make his country a great naval power. He personally designed the flag flown on the ships of this new navy, a blue diagonal cross, called a *saltire*, on white background.

It was at this time that the system in which a ship declared its nationality by flying an *ensign* at its stern and a *jack* at its prow came into general use. Today, most countires use their national flag as an ensign on both merchant ships and warships. Some countries, however, have different flags for different purposes. A number have a naval ensign which is different from their national flag; others, such as Israel, have a different merchant ensign. All British ships fly ensigns which are different from the national flag. Ships of the Royal Navy carry the white ensign, while British merchant ships fly a red ensign. A blue ensign is used by the Royal Naval Reserve, and, with the addition of badges and other devices, by a number of other special organizations.

In addition to the jack and ensign, warships also carry a long streamer flown from the mast, called a *masthead pennant*.

Flags bearing the traditional Sun Disc emblem appeared on Japanese warships during the 17th century.

International Signal Flags

One system of signal flags was agreed by the members of NATO, and uses 74 different flags. This includes flags representing the 26 letters of the alphabet, numeral flags, and 38 others. A similar, though less complicated system, was devised in 1927 for commercial purposes.

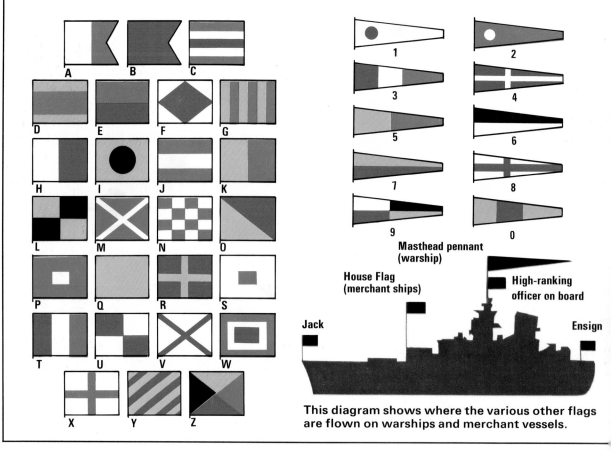

This diagram shows where the various other flags are flown on warships and merchant vessels.

Merchant ships carry a *house flag*, to show the identity of their owners. The use of these flags has a long history, and some modern designs are versions of flags first used as long ago as the time of Queen Elizabeth I. Today, house flags often take the form of an emblem seen on a ship's funnel. These emblems can refer to the history of the shipping line. For example, the P & O line uses the colours of the royal houses of Spain and Portugal, in recognition of the assistance given to the company by those families. Another example is seen on ships belonging to the Cunard line. They carry a red flag with a golden lion holding a globe, and below this, a red pennant with a white star. This refers to the fact that Cunard took over the old White Star line.

Ships of these lines often carry mail. When they do, a special white pennant is flown showing a crown and posthorn, and the words 'Royal Mail'.

When in port, ships are often decorated with the small coloured flags of the International Code of Signals. This system is also used to send messages at sea. The flags represent letters or numbers, and have special individual meanings. The flag for letter P is flown when a ship is about to leave port. The yellow flag for Q stands for 'Quarantine' meaning there is sickness on the ship.

Ships also make 'courtesy' signals with flags. For example, when any ship passes a warship, it will lower, or *dip*, its ensign in salute. When in a foreign port, ships fly the merchant ensign of the host country together with their own, as a courtesy.

Flags of the World

Today, every country of the world has its own national flag. In the following pages you will find these flags illustrated. They are arranged in groups, according to continent. In order to make it easy for you to find a particular flag, they have been numbered, from the first flag in Europe to the last flag in America. To find a particular country's flag, look for the name of the country in the alphabetical list below, where you will find it has a number. Use the number to find the picture of the flag.

► Somali women carry flags during a national parade.

Flags of Europe

1. Finland

2. Aland Islands

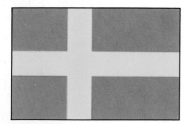

3. Sweden

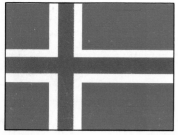

4. Norway

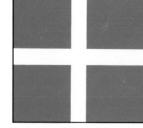

5. Denmark

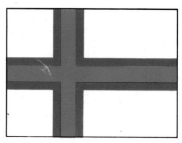

6. Faroe Islands

7. Iceland

8. Ireland

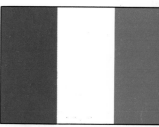

9. France

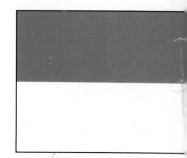

10. Monaco

11. Luxembourg

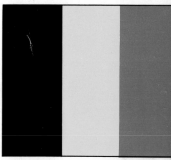

12. Belgium

Islands Around Britain

Isle of Man

Jersey

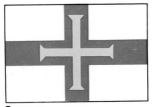
Guernsey

Alderney

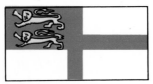
Sark

The Countries of the United Kingdom

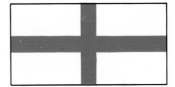
England

Scotland

Northern Ireland

Wales

3. Switzerland

16. United Kingdom

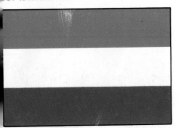
14. Netherlands

17. Austria

15. West Germany

18. Liechtenstein

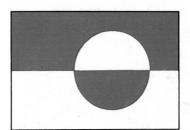
19. Greenland

13

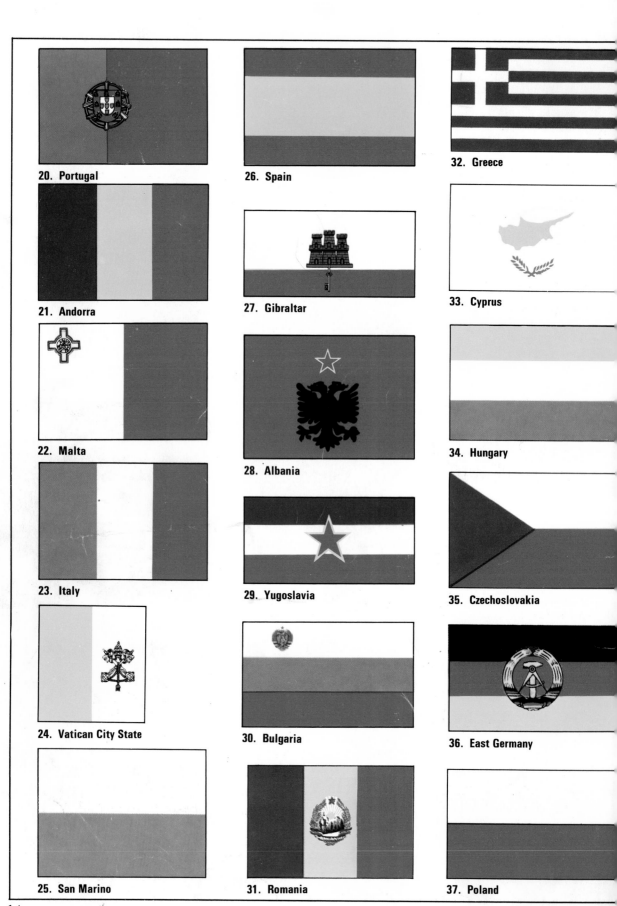

20. Portugal

21. Andorra

22. Malta

23. Italy

24. Vatican City State

25. San Marino

26. Spain

27. Gibraltar

28. Albania

29. Yugoslavia

30. Bulgaria

31. Romania

32. Greece

33. Cyprus

34. Hungary

35. Czechoslovakia

36. East Germany

37. Poland

The Soviet Union

38. Soviet Union

The official name of the Soviet Union is the Union of Soviet Socialist Republics. As this title suggests, the country is made up of many separate states, and each of these has its own flag. As you can see, these are similar to the national flag, but each has its own state colours or symbol in addition to the hammer and sickle. One of the most interesting is that of the Byelorussian SSR, which shows a piece of woven fabric on its left hand side.

Armenian SSR

Kazakh SSR

Russian SFSR

Azerbaijan SSR

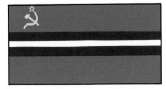

Kirghiz SSR

Tadzhik SSR

Byelorussian SSR

Latvian SSR

Turkmen SSR

Estonian SSR

Lithuanian SSR

Ukrainian SSR

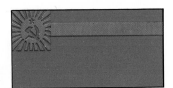

Georgian SSR

Moldavian SSR

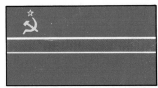

Uzbek SSR

Flags of Asia

39. Turkey

40. Syria

41. Lebanon

42. Israel

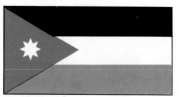

43. Jordan

44. Saudi Arabia

45. Oman

46. Yemen Arab Republic

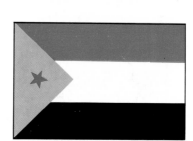

47. Yemen People's Democratic Republic

48. United Arab Emirates

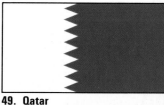

49. Qatar

50. Bahrain

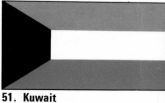

51. Kuwait

52. Iraq

53. Iran

54. Afghanistan

5. Pakistan

61. Bhutan

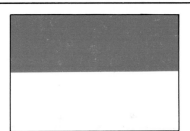

67. Indonesia

6. Bangladesh

62. Burma

68. Papua New Guinea

7. India

63. Thailand

69. Malaysia

8. Sri Lanka

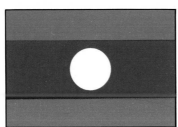

64. Laos

70. Singapore

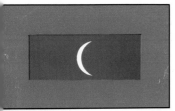

59. Maldive Islands

65. Kampuchea (Cambodia)

71. China

60. Nepal

66. Vietnam

72. Taiwan

73. Brunei

74. Mongolia

77. South Korea

75. Philippines

78. Japan

76. North Korea

79. Hong Kong

Flags of Australia and Oceania

80. New Zealand

83. Nauru

86. Solomon Islands

81. Guam

84. Kiribati

87. Tuvalu

82. Northern Marianas

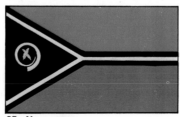

85. Vanuatu

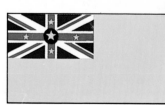

88. Niue

9. American Samoa

92. Fiji

95. Cook Islands

0. Western Samoa

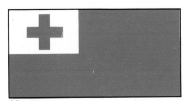
93. Tonga

96. Micronesia

1. Pitcairn Islands

94. Marshall Islands

97. Belau

Australian States

98. Australia

New South Wales

Tasmania

Queensland

Victoria

Northern Territory

South Australia

Western Australia

Flags of Africa

99. Sudan

104. Morocco

109. Mali

100. Egypt

105. Mauritania

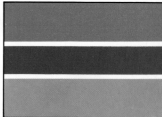

110. The Gambia

101. Libya

106. Senegal

111. Sierra Leone

102. Tunisia

107. Guinea-Bissau

112. Liberia

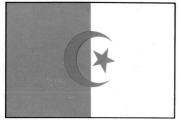

103. Algeria

108. Guinea

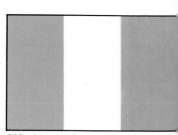

113. Ivory Coast

14. Burkina Faso

15. Ghana

16. Togo

117. Benin

118. Niger

119. Nigeria

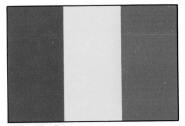
120. Chad

121. Central African Empire

122. Cameroon

123. Congo

124. Zaire

125. Equatorial Guinea

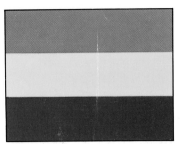
126. Gabon

127. Angola

128. Zambia

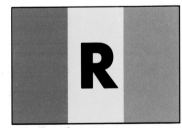
129. Rwanda

130. Burundi

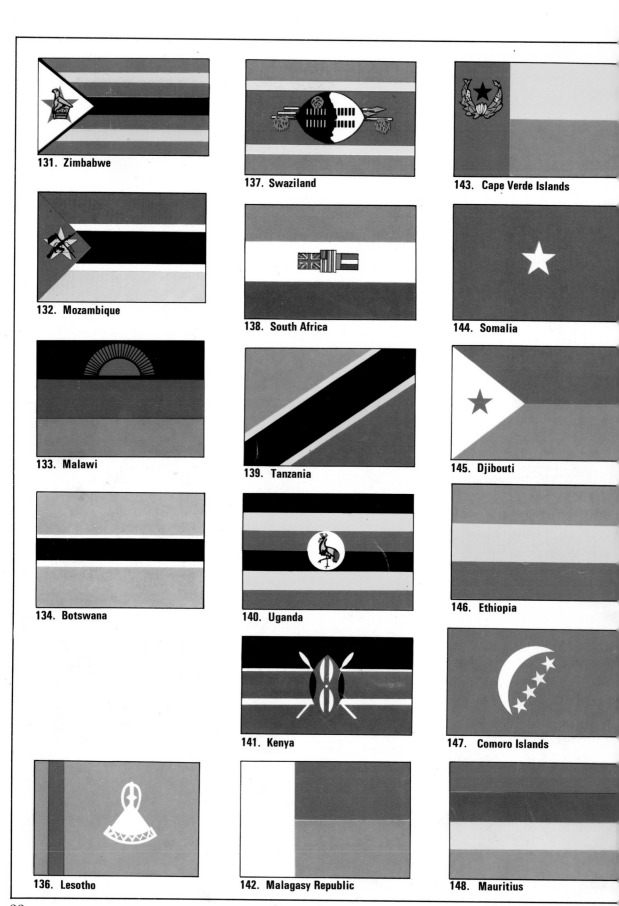

131. Zimbabwe

137. Swaziland

143. Cape Verde Islands

132. Mozambique

138. South Africa

144. Somalia

133. Malawi

139. Tanzania

145. Djibouti

134. Botswana

140. Uganda

146. Ethiopia

141. Kenya

147. Comoro Islands

136. Lesotho

142. Malagasy Republic

148. Mauritius

49. Seychelles

150. St Helena

151. Sao Tome and Principe

Flags of North America

Canadian Provinces

152. Canada

The provincial flags of Canada bear designs related to their separate histories. That of Quebec illustrates its association with France by showing a French *fleur-de-lis*; Nova Scotia's flag shows that province's origin as a Scottish settlement by carrying the royal arms of Scotland.

Alberta

New Brunswick

Nova Scotia

British Columbia

Newfoundland

Ontario

Manitoba

North West Territories

Prince Edward Island

Quebec

Saskatchewan

The Yukon

Flags of the United States of America

153. United States of America

Alabama

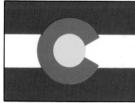

Colorado

The First Stars and Stripes

The first American Stars and Stripes was based on a rebel flag called the Continental Colours. It had a star and a stripe for each of the 13 rebel colonies. Two other rebel flags were the Pine Tree Flag and the Bedford Flag.

The Bedford Flag

Alaska

Connecticut

The Pine Tree flag

Arizona

Delaware

The Continental Colours

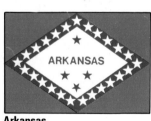

Arkansas

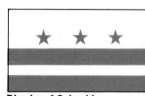

District of Columbia

The first Stars and Stripes

California

Florida

Georgia

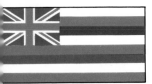

Hawaii

Idaho

Illinois

Indiana

Iowa

Kansas

Kentucky

Louisiana

Maine

Maryland

Massachusetts

Michigan

Minnesota

Mississippi

Missouri

Montana

Nebraska

Nevada

New Hampshire

New Jersey

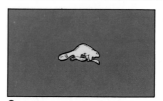

Oregon

New Mexico

Pennsylvania

Utah

New York

Rhode Island

Vermont

North Carolina

South Carolina

Virginia

North Dakota

South Dakota

Washington

Ohio

Tenessee

West Virginia

Wisconsin

Oklahoma

Texas

Wyoming

Flags of Central America

154. Nicaragua

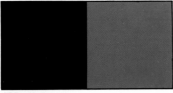

159. Haiti

164. Netherlands Antilles

155. Guatemala

160. Dominican Republic

165. Bahamas

156. Honduras

161. Costa Rica

166. Turks and Caicos Islands

157. Belize

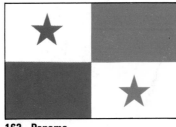

162. Panama

167. Puerto Rico

158. El Salvador

163. Antigua

168. Virgin Islands
(UK administration)

**168. Virgin Islands
(US administration)**

169. Anguilla (unofficial)

170. St Christopher Nevis

171. Cayman Islands

172. Jamaica

173. Cuba

174. St Lucia

175. St Vincent

176. Barbados

177. Grenada

178. Bermuda

179. Mexico

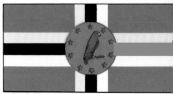

180. Dominica

181. Montserrat

Flags of South America

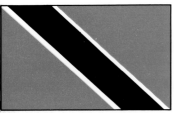

182. Trinidad and Tobago

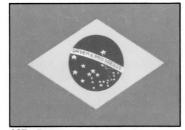

187. Brazil

192. Paraguay

183. Venezuela

188. Colombia

193. Uruguay

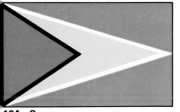

184. Guyana

189. Ecuador

194. Chile

185. Surinam

190. Peru

195. Argentina

186. French Guiana

191. Bolivia

196. Falkland Islands

National Flags

The state flag of France, 1640s–1790s

The Bastille flag, 1789

The revolutionary cockade of 1789

French national colours, 1790

The Dutch revolutionary flag

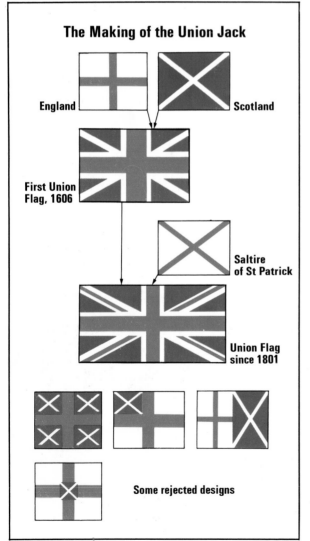

The Making of the Union Jack

England

Scotland

First Union Flag, 1606

Saltire of St Patrick

Union Flag since 1801

Some rejected designs

The development of modern national flags has often been associated with the political history of the country they represent. Revolutionary struggle, for example, has led to the creation of new national flags. The revolutionary flag of the Netherlands, a tricolour of orange, white and blue stripes, was flown during the 80-year Dutch rebellion against Spanish rule. The rebels' battle cry of 'Orange on Top!' referred both to their leader, William of Orange, and the flag they carried. During the French Revolution of 1789, the old heraldic flag of the monarchy was replaced first by the Bastille Flag and then by the French National Colours. The blue, white and red tricolour was seen for the first time in 1794.

The flag of the United Kingdom emerged as a result of the unification of the separate kingdoms of England and Scotland in 1603. The new ruler of both countries, James I, chose the first Union Flag in 1606. It took its modern form after the addition of the cross of St Patrick in 1801. More recently, in 1861, the unification of Italy led to the adoption of a national flag for the whole country, in the red, white and green tricolour.

As states have gained independence from foreign rule, so they have created national flags of their own. The flag of the United States

Mexico's Virgin of Guadalupe banner

The flag of unified Italy 1861–1946

A German unification flag, 1832

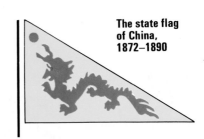

The state flag of China, 1872–1890

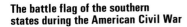

The battle flag of the southern states during the American Civil War

The banner of Oliver Cromwell

was first flown during the American War of Independence of 1775–1783. Early rebel flags included the Bedford Flag, and a red flag with a pine tree on a white rectangle in one corner. At the outbreak of war, the Continental Colours were flown, and this design later became the basis of the first Stars and Stripes. This flag had 13 red and white horizontal stripes, and 13 stars in a blue rectangle, one of each for the 13 rebel colonies. Today, there are 50 American states, and on the American flag there is one star for each of them, but the original 13 stripes have been retained.

Each of the American states also has its own flag. That of Hawaii bears a British Union Flag, although the reason for this is uncertain.

States and provinces within other large countries also have their own flags. Those of the Canadian provinces reflect their individual histories. Quebec's flag, for example, shows the French *fleur-de-lis*, and that of Nova Scotia the royal arms of Scotland. All but one of the Australian states flies a British blue ensign showing the state's badge.

Like the individual state flags, the Australian national flag illustrates Australia's origin as a British colony, by including the British Union Flag in its design.

The Arab Revolt flag hoisted in Jordan and Syria in 1918 and in Iraq the following year.

Alternative Russian civil flags used before 1914

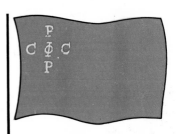

Russian national flag, 1918–1920

After the Russian revolution of 1917, red flags with gold inscriptions replaced the flags of the Tsarist regime.

West Germany, president

Israel, president

Guyana, president

Gabon, president

Personal standard of Queen Elizabeth II

Canada, Royal Standard

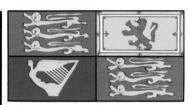
United Kingdom, Royal Standard

Australia, Royal Standard

Some Flags Flown by Queen Elizabeth II

United States, president

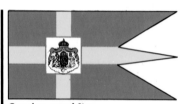
Sweden, royal flag

Japan, imperial flag

In some parts of the world, groups of countries all fly similar flags, as a result of common historical or political development. Tiny Luxembourg used to fly the same flag as its larger neighbour, the Netherlands, but in 1890 the blue horizontal stripe in its flag was made lighter in colour. In northern Europe, Norway was for centuries ruled by Denmark, and then later by Sweden. Iceland has been ruled by Denmark and Norway. As a result, the flags of Scandinavia have remained very similar in design.

In other areas, separate flags belonging to separate countries have merged when those countries have joined together. The modern Czech flag reflects the union of Bohemia, which had a red and white flag, and Moravia, whose flag was blue. Yugoslavia is a federal state, formed from states from Austria-Hungary and Serbia and Montenegro. The national flag incorporates the colours of the states out of which it was formed.

In monarchies, the king or queen often has an official flag indicating their status as head of state, separate from the national flag. This is called a *royal standard*. In some cases, such as Belgium, Denmark, Sweden, the Netherlands, Nepal and Thailand, these are based on the national flag, but show a royal coat-of-arms at the centre. The British monarch has a personal standard, and a separate royal standard for many of the countries in the Commonwealth.

National flags sometimes show political symbols as part of their design. In Germany in the 1930s, the rise of the Nazi Party led to the adoption of the *swastika* as a symbol. The flag of the Soviet Union is red, and shows a gold five-pointed star above a crossed hammer and sickle. The hammer and sickle are tools symbolizing the power of the manual worker, and are used as an emblem by the Communist government. The colour red is itself associated with Communism, and is the basis of the Chinese as well as the Soviet flag.

International Flags

In modern times, many flags have come to be internationally recognized. Perhaps the most famous and widespread of these are those used by the Red Cross, a neutral organization which provides medical aid throughout the world in times of war and disaster. The Red Cross Organization was founded at a conference in Geneva, Switzerland, in 1864, and was the idea of a Swiss citizen, Jean-Henri Dunant. Its first flag, a red cross on white background, was a reversed version of the Swiss national flag. This symbol has become internationally famous, on ambulances, hospitals and special hospital ships, protecting them from attack by military forces.

Some countries, who regard the cross as a Christian symbol, have other emblems for the same purpose. In Islamic states, with the exception of Iran, a red crescent on a white background is used, and in Israel the red cross is replaced by a red star, called the Red Magen David.

Another well-known international flag is that representing the United Nations. The UN was formed after the Second World War, in 1947, and its flag shows a white globe and white Olive wreaths on a pale blue background. The globe represents the organization's international status, and the Olive its ideal of maintaining world peace.

The United Nations is composed of countries from all around the world. Other associations of states also exist, and these have their own flags. The League of Arab States flies a green flag bearing a white crescent, symbolizing Islam, and the flag of the Organization of African Unity also contains the green of Islam. The flag of the Organization of American States shows a circle of linked national flags, to indicate the unity of its member countries. The Flag of the Race is flown in Spanish-speaking countries to symbolize the cultural links which exist between them. Another international flag is that of the Council of Europe, which shows a circle of 12 gold stars in the centre of a sky-blue background.

The flag seen at the Olympics reflects the games' aim of promoting friendship between all nations of the world. The five linked circles stand for the five continents of the world, and for the ideal of friendship. The device has been associated with the games since the first modern Olympics were held in 1906, and was first used on a flag in 1920, at the Antwerp games.

Red Cross

Magen David

Red Crescent

United Nations

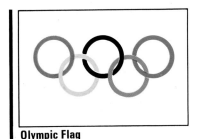

Olympic Flag

League of Arab States

Regional and Special Flags

In the early Middle Ages, the only people allowed to carry flags and banners were monarchs and the noblemen who formed their courts. The armies they commanded fought under these personal standards. Because the state was often closely identified with the monarch, the first national flags were often the personal flags of kings or queens. In the Middle Ages, associations of ordinary people began to be formed which were independent of a monarch or lord, and these often had their own distinctive flags. The development of regional and town flags is associated with these citizens' organizations.

Until the 11th century, the only flags carried by ordinary people were images of saints used at religious festivals or for protection in times of war. It was at this time that merchants, traders and craftsmen in some European towns began to form associations known as guilds which controlled the various local trades. Each guild, such as the goldsmiths, vintners or drapers, had an emblem, which it displayed on a banner.

In Austria, the province of Salzburg flies a flag with horizontal stripes in the colours of its medieval arms

It was also during the Middle Ages that regions began to assume their own identities and to create their own flags. The Swiss regions, called *cantons*, were among the first to do this, adopting heraldic designs on their flags. Similar banners were flown in the provinces of Belgium, the Netherlands, Norway, Austria and Germany, and later in the states forming parts of overseas territories such as Canada. The big trading ports of the Baltic and the Mediterranean also designed distinctive flags, which could be seen on their ships at sea.

Some Modern Regional and Town Flags

Hordaland province, Norway

The Glarus region of Switzerland

The province of Brabant, Belgium

Friesland, Netherlands

Paris

North Chungchong, South Korea

Kochi, Japan

Lower Saxony, West Germany

Helsinki

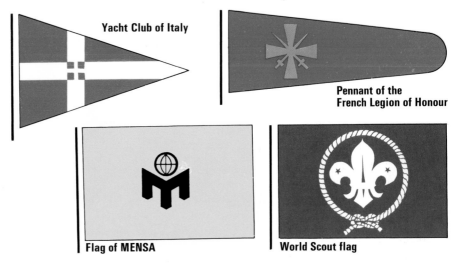

Yacht Club of Italy

Pennant of the
French Legion of Honour

Flag of MENSA

World Scout flag

Modern cities have their own individual flags, and many of these have long histories. The orange, white and blue tricolour of New York reveals the city's origins as a Dutch settlement. The blue and red flag of Paris became the basis of the modern French national flag during the 1789 revolution.

Special flags have for a long time been associated with armies, who used them to identify themselves. During the Crusades of the Middle Ages, the Christian army carried a red St George's Cross. This was also the emblem used by the English army in the period. The French army often used a white cross. More recently, individual regiments have had their own special flags, called *colours*. These commemorate victories or honours gained by the regiment, and can be very ornate, with decorative cords and tassels and other ornaments attached to them. Originally, colours were used to encourage troops during battle; today they are generally only seen on ceremonial occasions.

Many other organizations have their own special flags. These include sports clubs, particularly yacht clubs, whose members fly their own burgee, youth organizations such as the Scout and Guide movements, trades unions and other professional associations.

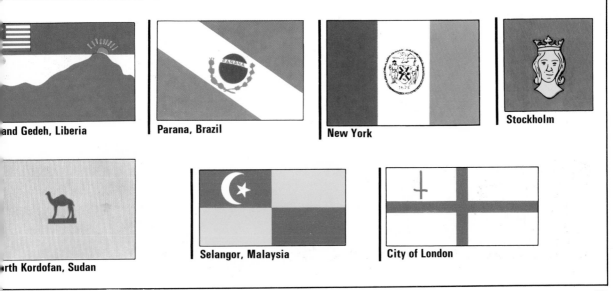

Grand Gedeh, Liberia

Parana, Brazil

New York

Stockholm

North Kordofan, Sudan

Selangor, Malaysia

City of London

Flag Design

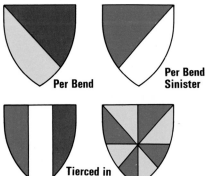
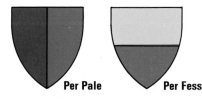
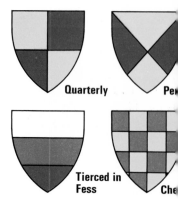

Per Bend **Per Bend Sinister** **Per Pale** **Per Fess** **Quarterly** **Per**

Tierced in Pale **Gyronny** **Tierced in Fess** **Che**

Heraldic Shield Partitions

The design of many flags seen in the western world today has been influenced by the patterns formed by partitions in heraldic shields. The names of these are shown here.

During the Middle Ages it became clear that a system was required to regulate flag design. Flags carried into battle by opposing armies during this period were almost meaningless as a method of identification. The Christian cross, for example, could be used by any of the armies of Europe. The dragon flag was equally common, favoured not so much as a means of identification as a weapon of terror.

The code of rules eventually adopted for flag design was known as *Heraldry*, and was associated with medieval family shields and banners. At the time of the Crusades, a knight would pass his shield on to his son, and with it the design it showed. These designs were gradually elaborated by heralds, who added *crests*, *supporters* and *mottoes* to them, and so created the impressive coats-of-arms whic reflected the social status of their owners. Th patterns and coats-of-arms found on a famil shield were then transferred to their flags an banners.

It was in this way that, by the middle of th 12th century, heraldry had come to regulat both shield and flag design. In 1188, a syster regulating the colours used by armies i Europe was also laid down, so that English French and Flemish troops could be distin guished by the colours of the flags they flew.

Most modern flags are rectangular in shape In the past, however, flags of many varie shapes have been flown, from the simpl triangular pennants attached to the lances c medieval knights, to the flags with strange tail

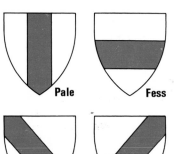

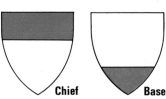

Pale **Fess** **Saltire** **Cro**

Bend **Bend Sinister** **Chief** **Base** **Canton** **Bord**

Simple Charges, or Ordinaries

The simple geometric designs called charges seen on heraldic shields have helped to create the designs of many of today's flags. Shapes representing various objects are also seen.

Flags are divided up into various geometrical patterns, consisting of horizontal or vertical stripes, rectangles, triangles and other shapes, all of which have special names.

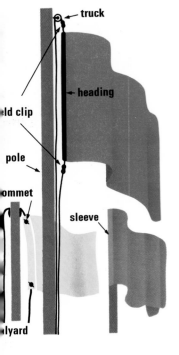

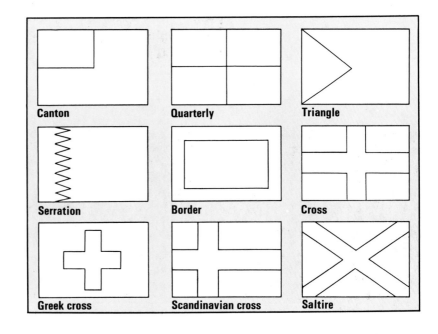

Canton	Quarterly	Triangle
Serration	Border	Cross
Greek cross	Scandinavian cross	Saltire

◄ The names of things used to hoist flags upon a flagpole are shown in this diagram.

and streamers flown in the countries of the East. In Europe, early flag shapes included the hanging *gonfalon*, a banner with tails attached to its lower edge, the *gonfanon*, a rectangular flag with broad tails along its flying edge, and the *schwenkel*, a rectangular flag with a long streamer flying from its upper right hand corner. One of the most famous flag shapes to have appeared in Europe is the *oriflamme*, a long tapering flag with tails.

Some of the most unusual flag shapes were found in the East, where, for example, the famous Mongol leader Genghis Khan carried a triangular banner decorated with yak tails, and with serrated edges called *flammules*. In Japan, the windsock was a common flag, and in Islamic countries the Islamic Banner was flown, a thin rectangular flag with a perforated edge.

Although the rectangle is now the most common of shapes, there are many colour patterns which can be employed in a flag's design, and these are based on the old heraldic patterns found on shields. A great many modern flags display simple horizontal or vertical stripes in various colours. Some flags include a small rectangle in the top left-hand corner. This is called a *canton*. The area containing the stars in the Stars and Stripes of the United States of America is a canton, as is that containing the Union Jack in the Australian flag. Other patterns include the division of the flag's area into four, called *quarterly*, and the triangle pattern, seen for example in the flags of Czechoslovakia, Guyana or Jordan. A zig-zag division, such as that seen on the flags of the Arab states of Bahrain and Qatar, is called a *serration*.

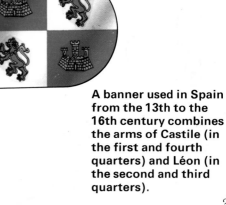

A banner used in Spain from the 13th to the 16th century combines the arms of Castile (in the first and fourth quarters) and Léon (in the second and third quarters).

Badges

Badges appear as emblems on flags. The Portuguese coat-of-arms appears as a badge on the national flag. The badge on Mongolia's flag combines the star of Communism with the Mongolian *soyonbo* symbol. Finland's coat-of-arms consists of a shield alone, and on the national flag the design appears in a shield of a different shape.

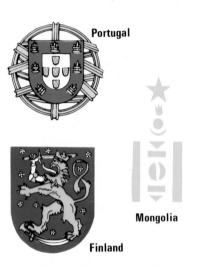

Portugal

Mongolia

Finland

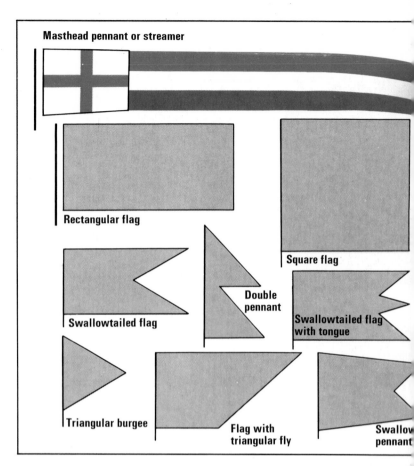

Masthead pennant or streamer

Rectangular flag

Square flag

Swallowtailed flag

Double pennant

Swallowtailed flag with tongue

Triangular burgee

Flag with triangular fly

Swallow pennant

In addition to shape and pattern, flags are also distinguished by symbols, and by their colours. Symbols used on flags can range from simple shapes, called *charges*, to complete coats-of-arms. Traditional charges include the *fleur-de-lis*, the eagle and the lion rampant. Modern charges can be seen in the maple leaf of Canada, or the straw hat which decorates the flag of Lesotho. Various kinds of cross appear on flags, including the St George's cross seen on the English flag, and the diagonal St Andrew's cross on the Scottish flag. Other symbols include the crescent moon of Islam, stars, suns, the hammer and sickle of the Soviet Union, animals, weapons and many others.

Colours may appear on flags for historical reasons, as in the case of the French flag, which adopted the red and blue of Paris during the revolution of 1789. Colours are also used because of their political or symbolic associations. Red has been taken to stand for danger and for Socialism, green for Islam, yellow for caution and for sickness, black for death, and white for peace, surrender or liberty. In Africa today, the colours red, gold and green in combination symbolize freedom and unity.

As flags have come to be regarded as emblems of authority and patriotism, some countries have made regulations to ensure that their flags are treated with proper respect. Some countries do not permit private citizens to fly the national flag, while others have strict laws governing its use. In the United States there are laws forbidding the showing of disrespect to the flag, whereas in the United Kingdom there are very few restrictions on the display of the national flag. The British flag is seen everywhere from shopping bags to tea mugs. It is important that one country treat the flag of another with respect: many international disputes have taken place over a real or imagined insult to the flag.

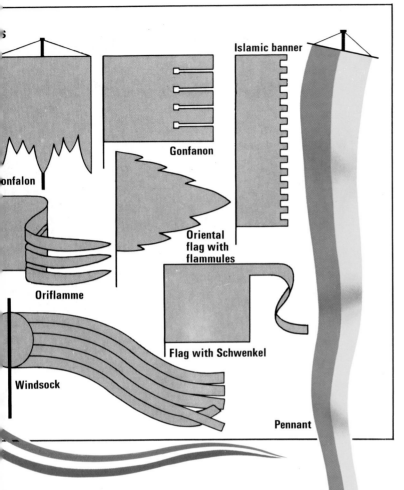

Gonfalon

Gonfanon

Islamic banner

Oriental flag with flammules

Oriflamme

Flag with Schwenkel

Windsock

Pennant

Bunting

Cockade

Edge Decorations

flammule

scallop

incision

fringe

Traditional Charges

Fleur-de-lis

Lion rampant

Eagle

Modern Charges

Maple leaf, Canada

Straw hat, Lesotho

Swords, Jordanian army

Zambia, president

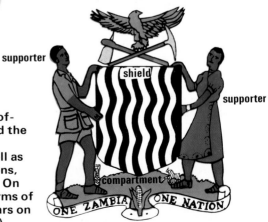

supporter

shield

supporter

compartment

scroll with motto

Some flags today bear complete heraldic coats-of-arms. The features around the shield all have symbolic meanings. Nations, as well as individuals or organizations, have such coats-of-arms. On the right is the coat-of-arms of Zambia, which also appears on the presidential flag (left).

39

Index

National flags of individual countries can be found by referring to the index on page 11.
Numbers in **bold type** refer to illustrations.

Acknowledgements

Photographs: cover Robert Harding Picture Library; 1 Zefa; 3 Robert Harding Picture Library; 5 Michael Holford; 8 National Maritime Museum; 9 British Museum; 11 Alan Hutchinson; 35 Transport and General Workers Union.